Floral Appliqué

Original Designs and Techniques
for Medallion Quilts

Nancy A. Pearson

This book belongs to

_____

Editing and production direction by Mary Coyne Penders.
Technical editing by Lenore Parham.
Illustrations by Nancy A. Pearson.
Cover concept by Nancy A. Pearson. Design by Jeff Bartee and Hani Stempler.
Book design and production by Character Place, Inc., Atlanta.
Photography by Sharon Risedorph, San Francisco.
Photograph of Nancy A. Pearson by Tony Cascarano.
Printing and color separations in China by Regent Publishing Services, Limited, Hong Kong.

First edition - Fourth Printing

Library of Congress Cataloging-in-Publication Data

Pearson, Nancy A., 1931-
        Floral Appliqué: Original Designs and Techniques for Medallion Quilts

        1. Appliqué   2. Quilt Design   3. Crafts and Hobbies

ISBN 1-881588-11-4

Publisher
P.O. Box 398
West Warren, MA 01092-0398
visit www.wrights.com &
www.ezquilt.com

DEDICATION

To My Grandchildren:

John, Melissa, Christine, Danielle,

Sean, Joseph and Mary Catherine

ACKNOWLEDGEMENTS

I would like to thank the following people for sharing their talents and participating in the creation of this book:

A special thank you to Mary Coyne Penders for all her encouragement, patience and careful editing. Without her, this book would never have been started or finished.

To Lenore Parham, who stitched the exercises and helped work through the problems.

To Marian Brockschmidt, Judy Elwood, Ulla Moe, Grace Pierson, Judy Roberts and Susan Scovern for sharing their wonderful quilts.

And especially to my good friend Lucille Daly, whose use of my designs in her quilts has brought me pleasure for many years.

TABLE OF CONTENTS

INTRODUCTION

While I was going to art school, I had an instructor who told me that I used my oil paints "like they were watercolors," so I took a watercolor class. The instructor for the watercolor class said, "You can't get texture with watercolor paints," so that was the end of my watercolor painting. I'm sure they would both shake their heads if they could see me now, trying to do my "painting" with fabrics. With a graphic arts career in my background, and several years of working with flowers and flower arranging, I suppose I was bound to combine these interests into quiltmaking.

It is exciting to see what can be done with fabrics and floral designs to create a completely individual piece of fiber art today. The possibilities are endless, which may be why painting with fabric is so successful with quiltmakers. This is also due to the large selection of wonderful fabrics available today. Painting with fabrics may not have been possible in the late nineteen-seventies and early nineteen-eighties, because the selection during those years was very limited. Will any of us who began quilting in those years ever forget those primary-colored calicos? Ugh!

My love of hand-appliqué and teaching has inspired me, with the help of others, to put this book together. I wanted to give you a guide to choosing color and fabrics, improving your hand-appliqué techniques and planning a floral medallion quilt. I've focused on several areas of floral appliqué design, including ideas for laying out a quilt design, and important information on how to create dimension by the placement of lights and darks within a flower.

Considerable space is devoted to basic stitching instructions, which should make hand-appliqué easier for you. If you read the instructions carefully, and try the stitching exercises, I am confident that you will find them helpful. I am especially pleased with the *Twisted Fabric* technique, which is used for stitching folded ribbons, leaves and other shapes with long, narrow points. I developed the technique out of necessity when I was appliquéing a Christmas design with lots of flowing and folding ribbons. I am sure it will help you too.

For many generations, floral patterns have been favorites of quiltmakers everywhere. I hope that the information in this book helps to perpetuate that tradition, and that the original floral designs presented here inspire you to create your very own special hand-appliquéd floral medallion quilt.

Nancy A. Pearson

Morning Glory by Nancy A. Pearson, Morton Grove, Illinois.
Quilted by Ruth Bell. 82" x 82". Collection of Nancy A. Pearson.

PART ONE

COLOR AND FABRIC: CREATIVE POSSIBILITIES

When you create a new project, you immediately think about which colors to choose. The selection you make is the single most important step. No matter how perfectly the piece is stitched, the project will not be a success if the colors do not work together to enhance the appliqué design. I have several ideas to help you make your color choices, whether you are a beginner or an experienced quilter or somewhere in between.

THEME FABRICS

Find a favorite piece of multi-colored fabric to use as a guide. I like to call this piece a *Theme Fabric* because it provides the color scheme for your whole project.

Pull all your colors from this fabric. *Do not add any colors that are not in the multi-colored fabric.* A Theme Fabric enables you to take advantage of the expertise of the fabric designer, and helps you feel more secure with your color choices. A good example of working with a Theme Fabric can be seen on page 78 with Ulla Moe's quilt *Flowers And Stars.* Notice how Ulla took the colors for this quilt from the border fabric.

Theme Fabrics are a source of pleasing color combinations for appliqué projects.

You can enlarge your selection by adding lighter tints or darker shades of any of the colors in the Theme Fabric. Look how effectively Lucille Daly has accomplished this with her quilt, *My Sister's Garden,* on the next page.

My Sister's Garden by Lucille Daly, Joliet, Illinois.
108" x 108". Collection of Cleo Albert.

Try using some of the Theme Fabric itself in your project. It might be used in the appliqué, or in the pieced border, or as a frame for the center block. Occasionally I've even used Theme Fabric for the background behind my appliqué. Look at how well Marian Brockschmidt used her Theme Fabric, in both the basket and in two of the borders, in **Marian's Rose Basket** on page 84.

BACKGROUND FABRICS

When choosing a background fabric for your floral appliqué, remember that this fabric determines the overall mood of your piece. Do you want to impart a Victorian aura to your project? Use one of the many white-on-white floral fabrics, which make beautiful backgrounds. For an example, look at my *English Garden Basket* on page 18. If you are looking for a soft, gentle, feminine feeling, try a very light pastel color. Remember that the background should complement the Theme Fabric.

I have discovered that placing floral appliqué on a dark background fabric, rather than the traditional light color, creates a dramatic feeling. The *Tulips On Black* pictured on the following page is an excellent example. My *Poppies* quilt, on the cover and on page 68, shows how clear, bright colors on a dark background also produce beautiful results.

Tulips on Black by Nancy A. Pearson, Morton Grove, Illinois. 18" x18". Collection of Nancy A. Pearson. Clear, bright colors on a black background produce stunning results.

Avoid using medium value fabrics for the background. It is too difficult to keep the floral elements from fading into the background. The contrast between colors is lost. Also avoid using a busy print for background, for the same reason that the appliqué pieces will not show up.

NANCY'S HELPFUL HINTS

I seldom cut away the background unless I feel that it is absolutely necessary. Most patterns have many small pieces and it is difficult to cut the background away from behind every piece. Also, I believe that the stability that the background fabric provides is very important. However, I will cut a dark background fabric away if the dark fabric shows through the light colored petals, or if I want to quilt a particular area.

FABRICS WITH "ZING"

The appliqué artist has the advantage over the painter in selecting colors. Because she is working with fabric, she is able to select many different patterns or textures for each color. Having a large selection of fabrics on hand is the best way to gain this advantage. Fabrics become your paints.

Because you cannot mix your fabrics to create a certain color, as a painter mixes pigments, you need a large collection of fabrics to help you "paint" your quilted picture. Fortunately, floral appliqué pieces are small, and do not require large amounts of any one fabric. Collecting small pieces means that you can make your fabric investment go much farther.

English Garden Basket by Nancy A. Pearson, Morton Grove, Illinois.
24" x 36". Collection of Nancy A. Pearson.

Here are some particular "paints" to look for when you shop for fabric.

Look for fabrics that have light and dark shaded areas within the same piece. This kind of fabric often contains several of the tints or shades you have in mind.

Look for hand-dyed mottled fabrics that have many light and dark areas. These fabrics add visual interest to petals and leaves. Examine the **Grapevine** piece below, and enlarged on page 51, where the highlights on the grapes come from the light spots on the mottled fabric. This creates a curved effect.

Look for wonderful, large floral prints. Cut your petals from their flowers, and your leaves from their leaves. This produces a charming effect for very little effort.

Inspect the wrong or back side of fabrics. Some prints may be solid on the back, giving you two choices for the price of one. Other fabrics may have the same print on the back, but with a much softer appearance. The use of both sides of a fabric can be especially effective in ribbons and multi-colored flowers. In the **Fan and Floral** quilt on page 36, the border around the center block and the outer border are border prints used on the wrong side.

Using both sides of fabrics extends your fabric
collection and multiplies your choices.

Many students ask me if I prefer using prints or solids. I like to mix
them because this multiplies my choices. To see how this works, select
eight different red fabrics, prints and solids, from your collection and
put them together. You'll notice that one solid might be a little more
pink than the others; a floral may give the illusion of a curved surface.
Another print has an interesting texture, while the addition of a geometric design provides a nice contrast. Plaids and stripes, used in
Country Basket on page 90, work well and are always a surprise to the
viewer.

Eight red fabrics display a range of
values and visual textures.

Use 100% cotton or silk fabric. The Appliqué "No-Baste" method requires the seam allowance to be creased under, and only a natural fiber will hold the crease. Silk has a wonderful sheen that cotton fabrics lack. A few pieces of iridescent silk, used with cotton fabrics, work wonders for flowers. Silk pieces are also very effective eye-catchers. Look closely at the ribbon and the fan in my *Fan and Floral* quilt on page 36. They are both silk fabrics. Notice that every other rib in the fan is silk. Many of the leaves and flowers in *Morning Glory* on page 12 are also silk. The introduction of the silk pieces adds a luster to the appliqué that is beautiful.

Silk fabric used for appliqué should have a lot of body. Try silk taffeta, Thai silk or heavy China silk. If you shop the merchant malls at the quilt shows in your area, you may find vendors who carry small packets of glowing silk fabrics. Local dress fabric shops are another source for silks.

NANCY'S HELPFUL HINTS

If you can't find eight values of one color in your collection to place together to "paint" a flower, this means that you need to look at values when you shop for fabrics. Make sure you include a selection of lights and darks, as well as mediums, so that you can "shade" effectively. The more time you devote to working with your fabrics, the more possibilities you will discover. The combinations are endless!

FOCUS AND BALANCE

Floral designs require colors that establish a focal point and lend balance to the design. Follow these recommendations to achieve this important aspect of color placement.

Place the brightest color in the main flower of the design. The strength of this color produces a focal point, the place where you want the eye to travel first.

If the bright color is placed in the center of the design, it does not need to be repeated elsewhere. When a color is used once on a design, that color acquires added strength, drawing the eye to that very spot.

Place a little of each color on both sides of the design. Don't keep one color on the right side, and another color on the left side.

Whenever possible, place each color at the points of an invisible triangle. Moving the triangle slightly for each color automatically balances the color of each flower group within the design. See how this works with **Urn With Roses, Calla Lillies and Poppies,** on the following page.

Urn with Roses, Calla Lilies and Poppies is a paste-up example by
Nancy A. Pearson, Morton Grove, Illinois. 23" x 23".

COLOR FAMILIES

To eliminate confusing the eye, it is important to give each flower family its own color. This means that a color is not carried from one type of flower to another. If you are working with a Theme Fabric, you will have a good source for finding many colors that work well together.

When a group of fabrics is assembled for a family of flowers, such as a large rose, a half-opened rose and a few rosebuds, they need to be tied together by the color and the fabrics. Look closely at the different flower families in my *English Garden Basket* on page 18; also see the irises and tulips in my *Flowers of the Summer Sun* on page 81. To achieve this effect, follow this simple rule:

Carry the color and a few of the same fabrics from one flower to another within the same flower family.

Sometimes the results of color choices are surprising and unusual. For example, I've seen beige roses, red jonquils, and even black daisies, all of which worked very well. Notice how effective the brown tulips are in Lucille Daly's *Garden Party* on page 38. See how Judy Elwood surprises the viewer with the unexpected, with her rendition of black tulips in *Black Parrot* on page 75. Remember that when you create a floral design you are creating a fantasy. Try these two ideas for your fantasy.

Combine two different colors within the same flower. Nature is the perfect role model. Just look at roses; there are combinations such as pale yellow with just a touch of pink, or red and peach.

Use different sizes and types of prints within each flower. Look at the variety used in Judy Roberts' *Fantasy* on page 29.

DIMENSIONAL SHADING

The illusion of dimension within the flowers is created by the placement of light and dark fabrics. The following rule will help you to achieve dimension. Keep this rule in mind when you are selecting and using fabrics, and you will be pleased with the effect it creates.

Light colors move forward. Dark colors move back within the flower.

Determine which petals are farther away, and make them darker. Make the petals which are closer a lighter value. Place a bright fabric somewhere between them, in one of the petals, which is a good way to catch the viewer's eye. The large flower in my **Flowers of the Summer Sun** quilt on page 81 is a good example.

To make a rose, a lily, or a similar flower look deep in the center, try using some dark fabric on the inside. Then, as the flower begins to open up, let the fabrics become lighter. Experiment! You'll like the results. See how this is done in my **Poppies** quilt on page 68. The blue jonquils in Lucille Daly's **My Sister's Garden** on page 14 are another example.

Pasting up a flower or a block provides a preview of the finished product
and allows for easy changes to be made.
Can you tell which rose is stitched and which rose is pasted?

Often I make a fabric paste-up of a flower to work out the best effect. First I cut the pieces of the flower out of fabric without adding seam allowances. Then I glue the pieces down on paper in the order in which they would be stitched. This method gives me a good idea of what the flower looks like without having to do any sewing. As you see in the photograph (page 25), the paste-up flower and the sewn flower appear to be identical.

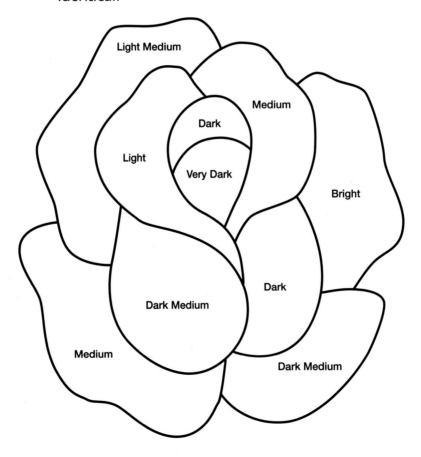

Shading the Rose. Use this diagram of the rose to discover how shading for dimension works.

Follow these easy steps for dimensional shading:

1. Cut out templates for the rose and mark the shading on them. When two petals are marked with the same value, use two different fabrics in that value. Petals of the same value should not be made from the same fabric.

2. Trace the drawing of the rose on a blank sheet of paper.

3. Select ten fabrics of one color, in solid or printed fabrics. Shade the fabrics from very dark to light.

4. Place templates on the corresponding pieces of fabric and cut out without adding a seam allowance.

5. Place the fabric pieces on the tracing of the rose. Look carefully as you ask yourself these questions:

    Do all the fabrics work together?
    Are some of the fabrics too busy?
    Is there enough space between the shades?

6. Arrange the pieces until you get a combination you like. Then paste down to make the completed flower.

LEAVES AND STEMS

While planning the color for leaves and stems, care must be taken not to let them overpower the flowers. The stems and leaves act as support for the flowers and tie the design together.

Judy Roberts' **Fantasy** displays a variety of greens for leaves and stems. Compare the effects of the dark and light backgrounds on the various colors and design elements. Keep the following guidelines in mind when you are choosing fabrics, and you will enhance the design.

For working on a dark background: the larger the leaf, the darker the color. As the leaves get smaller, they become lighter or brighter.

For working on a light background: the larger the leaf, the lighter the color. As the leaves get smaller, they become darker. To see how this works, look at the **Urn with Roses, Calla Lillies and Poppies** on page 23. Imagine that the large leaves are dark; then you can visualize how the leaves would overpower the flowers.

The balance of color and the size of the print are two elements to focus on; they rule the selection of fabrics. Here are some suggestions to help you with your choices:

It is not necessary to use the same fabric in all the same shaped leaves. In fact, more interest is created by the use of many different fabrics, as displayed in the **Fantasy** block on page 29. When using different fabrics for the leaves, make sure that their color intensity is the same.

When there are two large leaves, one on each side of the design, use the same fabric for each one. This achieves that all-important balance, and it will be pleasing to the eye.

Fantasy by Judy Roberts, Kansas City, Kansas.
18" x 18". Collection of Judy Roberts.

A printed fabric containing curved elements will line up with the curved shape of the leaf producing a wonderful effect. Notice how the leaves in the bottom center of *Flowers of the Summer Sun* on page 81 follow the contour of the fabric.

Try mixing different hues of green together. Blue-greens, true greens and yellow-greens all work well together. This is what happens in nature!

Whenever possible, use one print that contains all the different greens mixed together. This type of print helps tie all the green fabrics together.

Here are some additional guidelines for choosing fabrics for the stems:

Stems should be a strong, contrasting color, bright enough to be seen easily on both dark and light backgrounds. If you have chosen a range of greens for leaves and stems, use the darker green for narrow stems when working on a light background. Notice how visible the stems are in my *Morning Glory* quilt on page 12, even though the background color changes.

Use prints as well as solids for stems, and be sure that the color intensity or brightness is the same. A bright color can be as intense as a dark color, and when they are used together they balance one another and create interest for the eye.

Avoid using geometric fabrics for the stems. If the print is not printed on the true bias, it is not possible to line up the stems on the print and still cut on the true bias.

NANCY'S HELPFUL HINTS

Because one side of the seam allowance for the stems is trimmed very close, I recommend using cotton fabrics for these narrow pieces. Synthetic fabrics are more likely to fray or pull away from the stitching.

RIBBON ILLUSIONS

I want to make the viewer think that the ribbons in my floral appliqué quilts are actually twisting and turning. This is an illusion, of course, and must be planned. Look carefully at the ribbon in the design to determine which is the right side and which is the wrong side of the ribbon as it twists, or which parts are farther back and which parts are closer to the viewer. Place the lighter values on the right sides, or parts of the ribbon nearer the viewer, and the darker values on the wrong or far sides.

Nancy's Ribbon. This twisting, turning ribbon illustrates how light values move forward and dark values move back.

See the elaborate loops of the ribbon in the photograph and observe how the values are placed. I love to use ribbons in my work, and many of my pieces have multiple loops, bows and curls. Look at the ribbons in my *English Garden Basket* on page 18, and in Lucille Daly's *Portrait of Summer* on page 33 for additional examples. Notice also the handle on the *Country Basket* on page 90.

Remember that too much strong color confuses the eye. Multi-colored or busy printed fabrics also result in confusion. Instead, use one-color prints or tone-on-tone fabrics. Sometimes the soft or muted look of the back of a fabric may be a good choice for one of the sections. The ribbon is the last element that the viewer should notice. Ribbons work best as a support for the flowers and leaves, instead of competing with them.

This concept is also useful for leaves and petals. The illusion of a turned leaf or folded petal can add just the touch that makes a beautiful wreath or bouquet really outstanding. Many of the long leaves in my **Morning Glory** quilt on page 12 are twisted or folded. This heightens the graceful, flowing quality of the appliqué design. Just remember, to create a successful illusion of dimension, place the values according to the following rule:

Light values advance or move forward.
Dark values recede or move back.

BASKETS AND OTHER MOTIFS

Floral appliqué designs often contain baskets, bowls or urns. These are supporting elements and should never overpower the flowers. Be careful not to use too light a color, or from a distance the color will fade, the shape will disappear, and the flowers will look like they are floating on the background.

Baskets are good places to use a Theme Fabric, as I have done in my **English Garden Basket** on page 18. All of the colors in the block have been taken from the Theme Fabric, which I have used as the lightest fabric in the large basket.

Notice how the basket appears to curve. The darkest part of the handle looks farther back and the lightest section looks closer to you. The darkest part of the basket is on the outside, and the fabrics get lighter as your eye moves to the center. Placing the three fabrics in this order creates a dimensional look. Experiment with your fabrics to produce this effect. The same rule you learned for flowers applies to baskets:

Light values move forward.
Dark values move back.

Portrait of Summer by Lucille Daly, Joliet, Illinois.
86" x 108". Collection of Tracy Panepinto.

Sometimes, when using a shallow bowl or basket, I prefer a different look and will use a border print horizontally. The pattern of the fabric adds interest to the design, and also reinforces the long line of the container.

A fan can also be an attractive addition behind the central spray of flowers. To make the fan appear to fold, as in my *Fan and Floral* quilt on page 36, use two contrasting fabrics in the ribs. One of them might be your Theme Fabric, and the other a contrasting color or tone-on-tone print. Be careful not to use strong colors that compete with the floral elements.

BALANCE AND EFFECT

Now is the time to take a good look at your design and move things around until you are pleased with the effect. Do not start stitching any pieces down until you have experimented with placement!

When working on a project like a big multi-colored wreath or a large basket of flowers, I like to cut out the paste-ups and arrange them on the pattern, moving the flowers and leaves around to achieve the effect I want. This movement is of colors only, and does not affect or change the pattern.

I use this same method to plan colors for the ribbons. This means that you can put all the elements together without sewing them, and see how the finished product will look. Keep in mind as you go through the process that you are painting with fabrics.

Follow this checklist to help you see what works and what does not. Stand seven to ten feet from your paste-up so that you can look at it from the same distance as it will be viewed when completed and displayed. When you are satisfied, you will be ready to cut all the pieces and begin stitching.

Is there too much of the same color in one spot?

Are the leaves or stems too light or too dark?

Are there two prints next to one another that don't work?

Do any of the appliqué fabrics fade or disappear into the background?

PART TWO

PREPARATION: NECESSARY STEPS

FABRIC PROCESSING

Wash cotton fabrics before using them. Machine wash on a warm cycle, which will remove the sizing and take care of any shrinkage. Watch to see if the color bleeds. If this occurs, continue to rinse until the water runs clear. **If you can't stop the dye from bleeding, do not use this fabric.** I wash my fabrics without detergents, and I dry them in the clothes dryer on a low heat setting.

Perhaps you want to pre-wash silk fabrics. I believe that washing takes away some of the luster, but if you intend to wash your quilt then you will probably want to pre-wash the silks. Experiment with hand-washing a small piece and see what happens. In addition, don't press with a hot iron, or you will discover that heat does strange things to silk.

TOOLS AND SUPPLIES

I'm going to give you some recommendations for the tools and supplies I like to use for floral appliqué work. However, some of these items are widely available in various forms, and you must decide which needle or what kind of thread or marking pencil works best for you. Experience is the best guide.

I use size 10 milliner's or straw needles, which are very long and fine. I use cotton thread with cotton fabric and silk thread with silk fabric. I especially like the 100% cotton machine embroidery thread for appliqué. DMC and Mettler are good choices. My scissors are small with very sharp points. Because I pin from the back, I like long, fine silk or **Iris** straight pins.

Fan and Floral by Nancy A. Pearson, Morton Grove, Illinois.
Quilted by Karin Appel. 48" x 48". Collection of Mary and Steve Pyke.

I have found that a mechanical pencil works well for marking light colored fabrics. For dark colors, or silk, I use a white **Berol Prismacolor** pencil. I also use **Saral®**, a special transfer paper, for marking dark fabrics.

TEMPLATES AND PATTERNS

Templates for floral appliqué are cut to the finished size. When I make a set of templates for a project, I usually work with a plastic sheet made especially for this purpose. Sometimes I use good bond typing paper or a high grade of vellum. Your best choice is a material that shows pattern lines underneath. Follow these easy steps to produce a set of floral templates:

1. Draw the templates by tracing the pieces from the pattern onto the plastic. Accuracy is very important here. I use the black **Pilot®** permanent ink pen with an extra fine point.

2. Mark the corresponding number from the pattern to the template. The numbers represent the sewing sequence. There will be times when several flowers of the same shape will be sewn at different times in the sewing sequence. Remember to mark all the numbers on the templates so that you can identify the place in the sequence where each piece will be sewn.

3. Mark templates that will be used on the reverse side with the number followed by an "r."

4. Remember as you trace around the template onto the appliqué fabric that you are marking the finished size. Add an additional 3/16" seam allowance as you are cutting the fabric.

Garden Party by Lucille Daly, Joliet, Illinois.
86" x 86". Collection of Nancy A. Pearson.

sometimes pucker from side to side. Even though I have seen this happen to appliqué pieces time and again, I still pick up books with directions that insist on cutting on the straight of grain. Remember to cut on the bias!

3. Draw around the template with a sharp pencil. I use a mechanical pencil for marking light-colored fabrics, and the white *Berol Prismacolor* pencil for marking dark fabrics. The white pencil has a soft lead and needs to be kept sharpened. Drawing around the template with a dull, worn-down pencil adds size to the shape, and accuracy is lost.

4. After marking the shape on the fabric, cut out the piece, adding a 1/4" seam allowance.

5. Never use a lead pencil for marking on silk! The pencil line may smear. I use the white *Prismacolor* pencil for marking on silk.

NANCY'S HELPFUL HINTS

Many of the appliqué pieces are very small and easily misplaced, lost, or confused with other pieces. I mentioned before that I like to use small plastic bags to keep track of pieces. One bag for each flower helps keep the pieces in order.

HOW TO RE-MARK
THE PENCIL LINES

When appliqué pieces overlap, portions of the design marked on the background may be lost under the layers of fabric. This is easily remedied by re-marking.

1. When a piece is stitched so that it covers the pencil lines for the next piece, use the template for that shape to draw the pencil line onto the new fabric. For example, if piece "B" is stitched over the top of piece "A," stop sewing before you reach the line for "B." Take out the template for "B," line it up over the pencil lines, and draw the line for "B" onto the "A" fabric. See the illustration at the top of page 43.

2. Continue to re-mark each time a pencil line is covered over, so that the design is always moved onto the new fabric.

Detail from Fan and Floral (page 36).

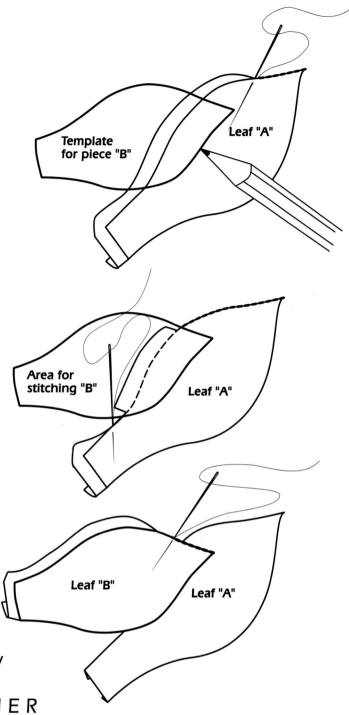

HOW TO SEW ONE PIECE OVER ANOTHER

1. Clip the "A" seam allowance just inside where "B" will be sewn down. Flatten out the clipped seam allowance. Continue sewing until you reach the flattened seam allowance. Take a running stitch across the "A" seam allowance, and finish sewing the leaf with the blind stitch.

2. Sew "B" in place over the top of the pencil line drawn on the background and also on piece "A." Now you have sewn down one leaf over the top of another without creating a ridge underneath.

THE NO-BASTE METHOD

Wouldn't you like to replace tedious basting with an easier method? The traditional method for appliqué requires two steps: first, the seam allowance of the appliqué piece is turned under and basted to itself; second, the basted piece is sewn to the background. Because I found this method very time consuming, I experimented until I developed the "No Baste" system, which is much faster and more accurate.

With the "No-Baste" method, a thumbnail crease is made along the pencil line, turning under the seam allowance on each piece. Then the pieces are pinned in place over the design which has been marked on the background. When you use my "No-Baste" method, you gain two advantages: making thumbnail creases eliminates time-consuming basting, and marking the design on the background ensures accurate placement of each piece.

Detail from **Morning Glory** (page 12).

HOW TO MAKE
A THUMBNAIL CREASE

1. Work with only one-half inch at a time.

2. Turn under the seam allowance on the pencil line, and place the
    fold on your left forefinger.

3. Using your left thumbnail, crease the fold firmly.

4. Continue working around the piece, folding and creasing as
    you go. Take small strokes when creasing, 3/8" to 1/2" at a time.
    The fabric will not stretch out of shape when you crease with short
    strokes.

5. When the piece is completely creased, gently flatten out the seam
    allowance. Pin in place carefully over the pencil lines marked on
    the background fabric. Correct placement becomes easier with
    experience.

Using short strokes, crease firmly with left thumbnail.

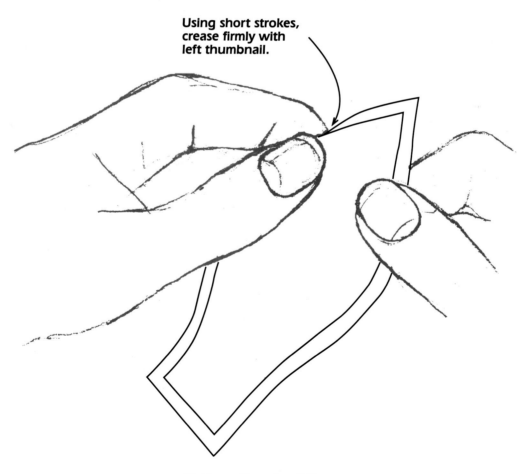

Making a Thumbnail Crease

NANCY'S HELPFUL HINTS

In tightly curved areas, make smaller creases, and let the creases overlap a little. Because the fabric I use is a 100% natural fiber, it has a memory. This memory will find the crease as you turn under the seam allowance to sew the piece down, giving you more control over the shape.

When pinning a piece to the background, pin from the back so that the thread will not catch on the pins as the piece is being sewn down.

Crease each piece before sewing, or crease several at a time, whichever you prefer. Crease before clipping curves.

To remove pencil lines, I use a fabric eraser and masking tape to take up the residue. For stubborn pencil marks, you may also want to try the following formula which I found in **Quilter's Newsletter Magazine** several years ago:

> Use three parts rubbing alcohol to one part water, with a few drops of clear dishwashing detergent.

White pencil usually wears off easily, but if you have a problem, try placing transparent tape on the line. Then rub over it with your thumbnail.

SEWING ORDER

Put the pieces down on the background in the order of stitching them. The patterns in PART FIVE are numbered in the correct stitching order. If you are already keeping track of the appliqué pieces in zip-lock bags, make a trial layout and then, when you are satisfied with the arrangement, put the pieces back in the bags until they are needed for stitching.

The center block from **Fan and Floral** (page 36).

Techny Chimes by Nancy A. Pearson, Morton Grove, Illinois.
Quilted by Karin Appel. 52" x 52". Collection of
Rush Presbyterian – St. Luke's Hospital, Chicago, Illinois.

PART THREE

STITCHING: SPECIAL TECHNIQUES

THE BLIND APPLIQUÉ STITCH

It is important that stitches do not show on appliqué work. Here is the technique I use for achieving a blind stitch. Experiment with the stitch on a piece of practice fabric first. As soon as it looks invisible, you are ready to begin sewing your appliqué pieces to the background.

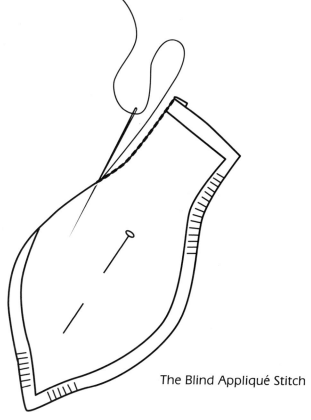

The Blind Appliqué Stitch

1. Fold the seam allowance under and crease with your thumbnail along the pencil line. Crease each piece completely.

(continued)

2. Place the knot out of sight, between the two fabrics.

3. Bring the threaded needle to the top of the appliqué, keeping the stitch as close as possible to the fold of the fabric. Work with the fold toward or away from you, depending on your preference.

4. Take the threaded needle over the edge of the fold, and down into the background fabric, directly across from where the needle came up.

5. Move over on the back and then up through all three fabrics, being careful that the stitches do not show.

6. Bring the needle over the fold again, moving the stitching along on the underside of the appliqué.

NANCY'S HELPFUL HINTS

Keep the stitches small, about ten stitches to the inch. This size means that the stitching should be secure through many washings.

Be careful to keep the fold of the appliqué shape directly over the top of the pencil line drawn on the background as the sewing continues.

Whenever the piece being sewn down will be partly covered by an overlapping piece, the seam allowance of the bottom piece needs to be clipped and flattened. This easy trick eliminates the creation of unsightly ridges where pieces overlap.

STEMS AND ENDS

Fabrics for narrow stems or vines should be cut on the diagonal or bias so that the fabric can stretch to follow the contour of the curves. Look at the narrow stems and curled tendrils in this photograph of the grapevine. To practice this technique, draw a gentle curve on a larger piece of background fabric. Use a 12" square of green fabric.

The curling tendrils of Nancy's **Grapevine** show the curves of the stems cut on the bias.

1. Fold back the corner of the stem fabric diagonally to find the true bias. The fabric should measure the same from the fold to the point on one side as it does from the fold to the point on the other side.

2. Crease along this fold with your fingertips.

3. Open up the fabric and draw the first line for the stem on this fold. If your fabric is dark, use the white pencil.

4. Move a ruler to the desired width of the stem and draw the second line.

5. Cut, leaving an extra 3/16" of fabric for the seam allowance on each side of the stem.

6. Crease under the seam allowance with your thumbnail along the pencil lines drawn on each side of the stem.

7. Open up and gently flatten out the seam allowances. Do not turn them under again until you begin to sew.

SEWING DIRECTIONS
FOR THE STEMS

1. Fold under a small section of the seam allowance along the pencil lines drawn on the stem fabric.

2. Line up the fold over the pencil line drawn on the background fabric.

3. Sew the inside curve (the shortest side) of the stem first, along the pencil line, using the blind appliqué stitch.

4. When you reach the end, stop and open up the seam allowance that has just been stitched down. Using sharp, pointed scissors, trim, leaving a generous 1/16" seam allowance. Be careful not to cut the stem.

5. Fold under the other side of the stem and stitch down. Using this method provides ample room for making the seam allowance flat and smooth.

When the end of the stem is not covered by another piece of appliqué, it will need a finished edge. This technique is also useful for making square corners on ribbons and baskets. To make a finished edge, follow these steps:

1. After thumbnail creasing the edges of the stem, make a crease across the end, creating a 3/16" seam allowance.

2. Cut off the corners of the seam allowance diagonally from one fold to the other. This helps get rid of some of the extra fabric at the corners, which makes folding under and squaring off the corners much easier.

3. Stitch the stem as previously instructed to near the end of the stem. Square off by folding the end under. Hold firmly and continue stitching to corner.

4. Place a small stitch in each of the folded corners to create a nice square end on the stem. Now fold under the other side, and continue sewing.

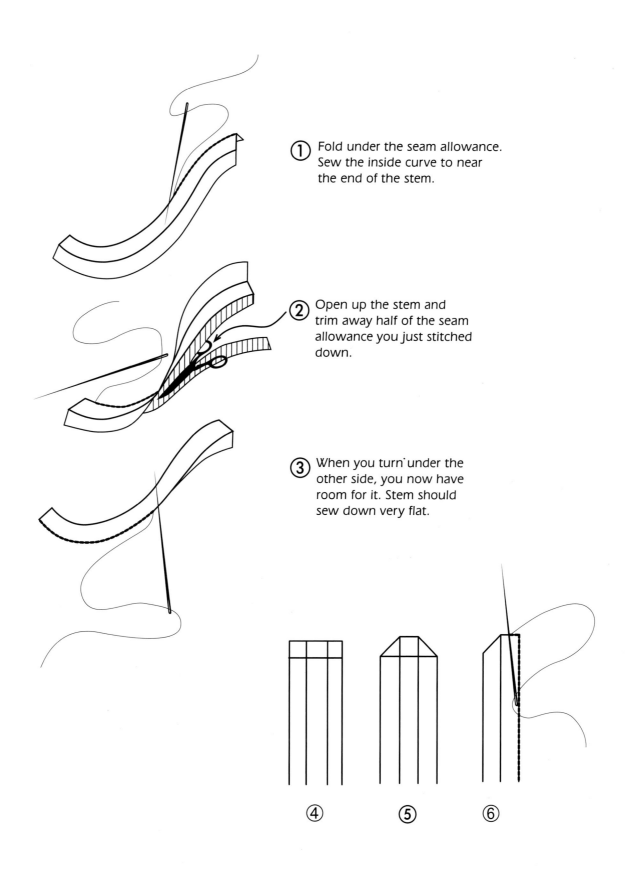

① Fold under the seam allowance. Sew the inside curve to near the end of the stem.

② Open up the stem and trim away half of the seam allowance you just stitched down.

③ When you turn under the other side, you now have room for it. Stem should sew down very flat.

④　⑤　⑥

LEAF POINTS

The challenge when appliquéing a leaf is to achieve a sharp, nicely shaped point. Try this method with a practice leaf.

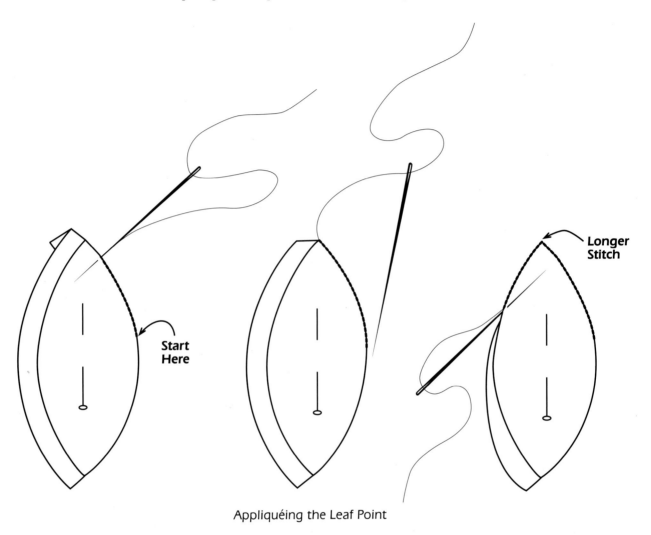

Appliquéing the Leaf Point

1. Cut out a template for a leaf. Draw around the template on both a piece of background fabric and the leaf appliqué fabric.

2. Add a 3/16" seam allowance to the fabric leaf as you cut it out. Crease under the seam allowance with your thumbnail along the pencil line around the shape, taking care to crease a nice, sharp point on the leaf. Pin in place from behind.

3. Begin sewing half-way down on the side of the leaf, stitching toward the point.

4. Keeping the seam allowance turned under, stitch to within 1/8" of the point and stop.

5. Fold under the seam allowance across the tip where the lines of the leaf form a point. Hold firmly so that it won't unfold.

6. Continue sewing, bringing the needle through the very tip. Take a slightly longer stitch here to create the illusion of a sharp point on the leaf.

7. Fold under the remaining side and continue sewing.

NANCY'S HELPFUL HINTS

Be sure to thumbnail crease the seam allowance before you start to sew. Then it will be easy to find that same crease along the fold as you sew, giving you more control of the shape.

Because the stitching begins and ends in a shallow curve on the side of the leaf, it is easy to tuck under the seam allowance. If the stitching begins at the point, this is difficult to accomplish.

Spring Blooms in My Winter Cabin by Susan Scovern,
Perrysburg, Ohio. 71" x 71". The outer border from June Ryker's
Log Cabin Rondelay was used to complete the center.

INSIDE POINTS AND OUTER CURVES

One of the most challenging aspects of hand appliqué arises with the inside point, which should be turned under without fraying. The inside point refers to the point at the top center of a heart or tulip shape. Try the following technique with a practice tulip shape, and you will learn how to eliminate the problem of inside points.

1. Cut out the tulip shape template and mark around it lightly on both a background and a flower appliqué fabric.

2. Cut the tulip shape from the appliqué fabric, adding a 3/16" seam allowance.

3. Crease under the seam allowance with your thumbnail along the pencil line around the tulip shape, making sure to crease a sharp point into the fabric at the inside point. To do this, fold under the seam allowance on the right side and, while creasing down into the point, fold under the left side, making it possible to crease into the point and beyond.

4. Open up the fabric and repeat the creasing of the left side in the same manner. This creates an "X" shape into the inside point. Sharply creasing this "X" helps guide you as you stitch the inside point.

The outer edge of the tulip shape has two concave curves. These curves must be clipped so that the seam allowance can fan open as it is turned under to be stitched. Clipping is done after the shape has been thumbnail creased.

1. Clip the seam allowance at a right angle to the pencil line.

2. Clip in about 3/4 of the way, making cuts every 1/16" for the length of the concave curve. Do not clip the outside or convex curves!

3. Pin the tulip in place over the top of the tulip drawn on the background fabric. Make sure that the inside points are placed one above the other so that they match.

NANCY'S HELPFUL HINTS

When points form as the seam allowance is turned under along the outside curves, it is a good idea to stop and trim some of the excess fabric away. Taking smaller stitches also helps to eliminate the problem.

PERFECT TULIPS

1. Begin sewing in the middle of the clipped area, on the right side of the tulip. (If you are left-handed, start on the other side.) Sew up and around the outer point, and over the top of the tulip. When you are about 1/4" away from the inside point, stop and take out the pins. Cut down into the inside point. See illustration "A."

    Take care to cut only to the pencil line, and not through it. Cutting too far often presents problems with fraying.

2. Following the "X" that was creased into the inside point, fold under the left side of the tulip and continue sewing until you get to the bottom of the inside point. Then, unfold the left side of the tulip, being careful to keep the seam allowance turned under, and finish sewing. You have made an inside point without any fraying. See illustration "B."

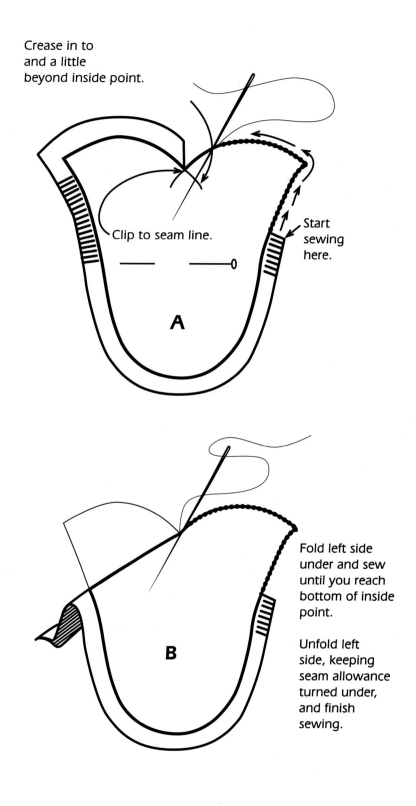

Crease in to and a little beyond inside point.

Clip to seam line.

Start sewing here.

A

Fold left side under and sew until you reach bottom of inside point.

Unfold left side, keeping seam allowance turned under, and finish sewing.

B

Perfect Tulips

PERFECT CIRCLES

Sewing a perfect circle has always challenged the fabric artist's skills. The challenge becomes easier to manage when you try following these rules on some practice circles:

1. Using a template, mark the circle clearly on the background fabric so that there is a line to guide you.

2. Cut out the fabric circle and thumbnail crease under the seam allowance around the edge of the circle. Make small creases and allow them to overlap so that the shape remains nice and round.

3. Do not clip the seam allowance. Instead, trim away the extra fabric, leaving about 1/8". Now the seam allowance will not pleat and form points around the edge as it is sewed down. In addition, taking smaller stitches will help you obtain a smooth edge.

4. Do not pin the circle in place. It is very difficult to line up the appliqué circle directly on top of the circle drawn on the background. Instead, take the first stitch any place along the pencil line. Keep moving forward, placing one pencil line over the top of the other, to produce the desired round circle. Remember that the circle drawn on the background functions as the guide to appliquéing a perfectly round circle.

5. While stitching around the circle, stop 1/2" from the end. Fold all the loose fabric under. Continue to sew using the point of the needle to pull out the fabric a little at a time, until it lines up with the pencil line. When you are a few stitches from the end, you will notice that the seam allowance is completely tucked under, and you don't have to struggle to get the last bits turned under.

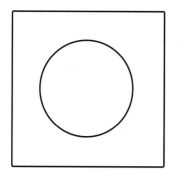

Clearly draw circle
on background fabric.

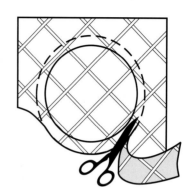

Thumbnail crease
around circle and
trim away extra
fabric.

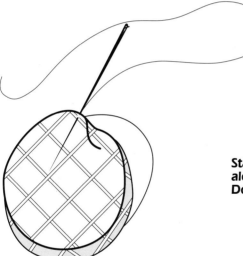

Start to sew anywhere
along the pencil lines.
Do not pin in place.

Tuck under last half
inch of fabric. With
needle, pull out fabric
as you need it.

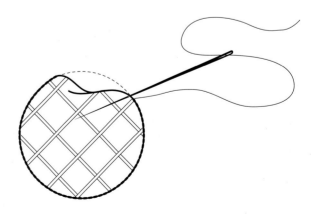

Sewing the Perfect Circle

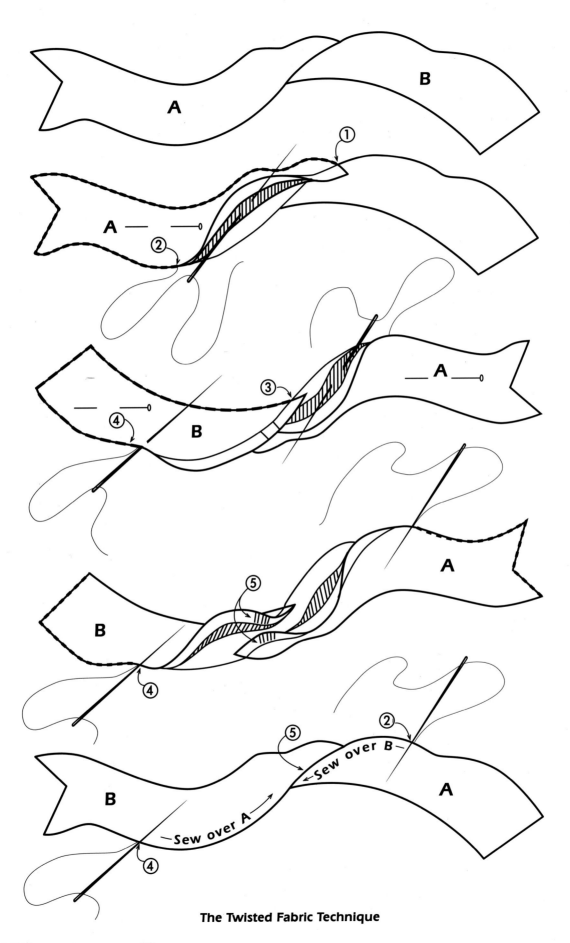

The Twisted Fabric Technique

THE TWISTED FABRIC TECHNIQUE

I developed this technique when I was searching for a way to appliqué a petal or leaf or ribbon that is folded over. Very often I was in a situation where I had to stitch long, narrow points where the petal or ribbon folds from one side to the other. I solved the problem with my *Twisted Fabric Technique*. Experiment with the technique by trying the following exercise, which takes you through the steps from start to finish. You will enjoy adding this unique feature to your stitching techniques.

1. Trace the two-piece ribbon shape onto a background fabric.

2. With matching templates, cut two pieces from contrasting fabrics, adding 3/16" seam allowance to each piece.

3. Crease under the seam allowance with your thumbnail along the pencil line around each piece. Remember to treat the inside point at the end of the ribbon the same as you treated the inside point on the tulip shape. Unfold the seam allowance and flatten.

4. Carefully pin piece "A" down, being sure it is lined up over the pencil lines on the background fabric.

5. To sew piece "A," start stitching at the top ①. Sew until you are a short distance away from where the two pieces meet. Leave the center edge open where it will be covered over by the other fabric. Stop and fold back the unstitched fabric. Hold it in place with the threaded needle and leave until later in the process ②. If you have difficulty sewing the sharp points of the ribbon, refer to page 54. For help with inside points, see page 57.

6. Pin piece "B" in place, lining it up carefully over the pencil lines. Turn the stitching exercise upside down. Thread another needle and start sewing piece "B" at the point ③.

7. Continue sewing around the outside edge until you are a short distance away from where "A" and "B" meet ④ . Notice that the outer edges are stitched down, and the inner edges are open. Move the threaded needles out of the way, and remove all pins.

8. Find the center area of the unstitched seam allowance ⑤, and clip these seam allowances opposite one another for about 1/4", making sure to clip every 1/16", and cutting into the seam allowance seven-eighths of the way. Fold under only the clipped areas and crease them with your thumbnail.

9. The two 1/4" edges are butted up against one another ⑤. Return to ④, and continue sewing piece "B" down, covering over the flattened edge of piece "A". When you reach the clipped area, sew to the middle, and then take the thread to the back. Knot and cut. Starting at ②, continue sewing piece "A," covering over the flattened edge of "B" until you meet stitching in the middle of the clipped area. Take the thread to the back, and knot and cut. You are finished! Notice that the fabrics are now twisted, or switched, in the center. You should not be able to see where the switch took place.

NANCY'S HELPFUL HINTS

Be sure the pencil lines on both fabrics line up, one above the other, where the two fabrics touch.

Detail of twisted ribbon from **English Garden Basket** by Nancy A. Pearson on page 18.

THE FINISHING KNOT

The finishing knot is a small, uniform knot to use for finishing off the thread on the back side of the work. The following instructions produce a square knot, which will not come undone when it is pulled tight.

1. Bring a threaded needle through to the back side of the fabric. Take a small stitch close to where the needle came through the fabric. (This results in a very small knot.) Push the needle half-way through the fabric and stop. Bring the single thread (the thread attached to the fabric) around and behind the point of the needle.

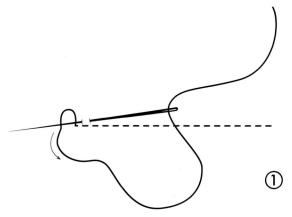

①

2. Bring the double thread (from the eye of the needle) around and behind the point of the needle in the opposite direction. Notice that the threads have crossed behind the needle point. Pull the threaded needle through, and a small knot will form against the fabric. Give the thread a tug to tighten it.

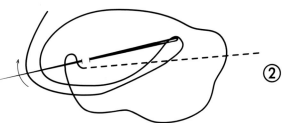

②

3. Go one step further and slip the threaded needle between the two fabrics, moving over a short distance. Pull the thread up through the fabric and clip. The tail will disappear between the fabrics.

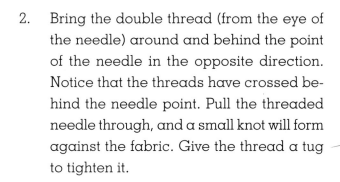

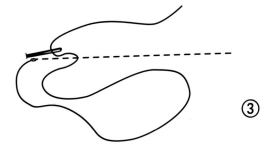

③

The Finishing Knot

NANCY'S HELPFUL HINTS

When you use the finishing knot, unsightly tails of thread will never show through from the back side of the piece after the quilting is completed.

EMBELLISHMENTS

Floral appliqué lends itself beautifully to embellishment. Embroidery has been widely used for many years by needleworkers to outline flowers and accent the curves of the petals. Floral appliqué provides abundant opportunities for the use of embroidery to accent the small details in the flowers.

Experiment with the many cotton embroidery threads available. Don't overlook your sewing threads, as they also can produce a lovely fine line. If you have access to silk embroidery thread, I urge you to try it. When used for French knots, silk embroidery thread adds dimension to the centers of the flowers. The wonderful luster adds something special to the flowers.

I always use a single thread because I like the fine, elegant look it gives. I especially like the outline stitch, and if you look closely at my *Poppies* quilt on page 68, you can see what a beautiful effect this embroidery stitch produces. I also used this stitch exclusively in my *Morning Glory* quilt on page 12.

Stuffed work and other special quilting stitches can also act as embellishments to your quilt. Extra batting or thick strands of yarn gives the floral elements or the quilted areas a dimensional appearance. Examine the quilting around the center motif in Judy Elwood's *Black Parrot* on page 75. Notice how the stipple quilting and the stuffed work combine to embellish the bird and flowers in the center block.

Detail of flower from **Poppies** by Nancy A. Pearson on page 68.

NANCY'S HELPFUL HINTS

Sometimes when you are sewing with silk fabrics or embroidering with silk floss, you might find that it snags on your fingertips, especially if your hands are a little rough. You can solve this problem with a tube of special cream called **Acid Mantle**. This cream works wonders, especially in cold weather; buy it from your local drugstore. Rub a little on your fingertips, and surprise, your fingertips are smooth and snag-free.

Poppies by Nancy A. Pearson, Morton Grove, Illinois. 40" x 40".
Collection of Nancy A. Pearson.

PART FOUR

DESIGNING: APPLIQUÉ MEDALLION QUILTS

Now you are ready to design your own floral appliqué medallion quilt. You will find it helpful to read this entire section first to gain an overview of the process. Then you can choose a pattern for the center of your quilt from the full-size patterns at the back of the book. All of these patterns are designed to be used in the center, with variations created for the borders.

LAYOUTS

Choose your layout from the four presented here, or design your own if you wish. The layouts are illustrated by black and white diagrams. Look at my quilts and the quilts made by my students to see how these layouts have been used. You can use them as presented, or change or combine them to suit the requirements of your piece.

The **Quilt Layout with Eight-Pointed Stars** on the next page demonstrates how sections of a pieced eight-pointed star can be used to support a center block that is set on point or on the diagonal. Try using two different shades of fabric to create a dimensional look in the stars. A combination of light or neutral colors is the best choice. Ulla Moe's **Flowers and Stars** on page 78 illustrates this very effective layout.

Additional appliqué can be used in the triangle shapes or in the outer border. Be sure to repeat the same background fabric that was used in the center block.

Notice how Ulla uses **Feature Strips** to divide the sections of the quilt. Keeping the **Feature Strips** the same color throughout the quilt helps to maintain continuity.

Quilt Layout with Eight-Pointed Stars. Scale: 1/4" = 2".

The shapes of the fan design in the **Quilt Layout with Fans** on the next page gently draw the viewer's eye to the center block. With this design, the block may be set on the straight or on the diagonal.

Be careful to keep the fan-shaped pieced work light in color so that it does not detract from the center appliqué. Notice how nicely the pale pink fabric works in Grace Pierson's *Tribute to Nancy Pearson* on page 92. This treatment supports the center, but does not detract from it.

Additional appliqué may be added in the outer corners. Keep the background fabric under the appliqué the same.

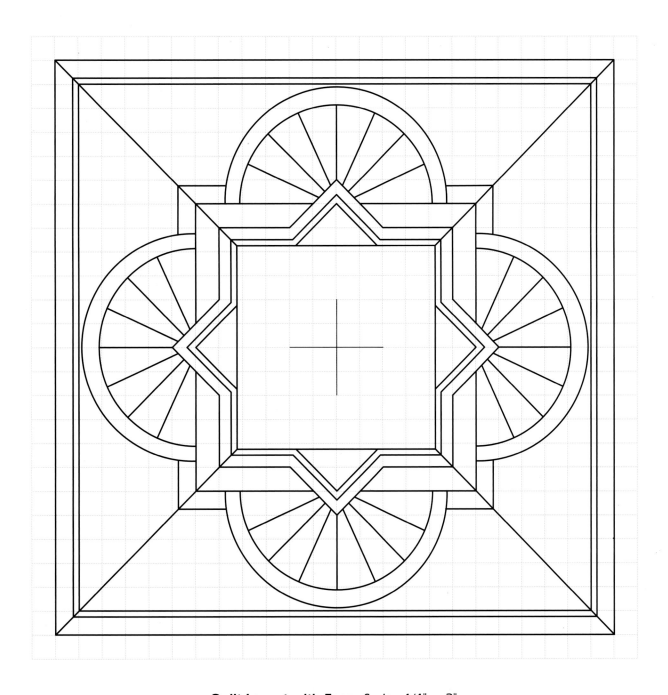

Quilt Layout with Fans. Scale: 1/4" = 2".

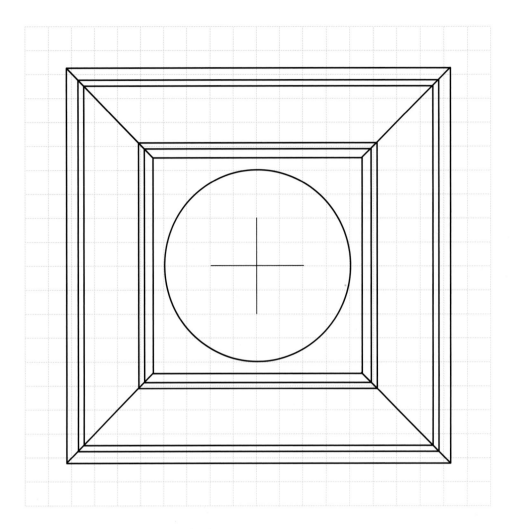

Circle within a Square Layout. Scale: 1/4" = 2".

The Circle within a Square Layout may be adjusted to fit any size block. Try using your **Theme Fabric** in the area behind the circle, or in the border. It is not necessary to use more appliqué in this layout because there is only one border. If you decide to use additional appliqué, keep it very simple and supportive.

Look at **Flowers of the Summer Sun** on page 81 to see how beautifully this simple treatment complements the appliqué.

The Octagon Quilt Layout is versatile. The octagon shape easily lends itself to blocks done on point and to blocks done on the square. Marian Brockschmidt's use of a dark border print works nicely to frame the appliqué in the center of **Marian's Rose Basket** on page 84. Try edging these pieces with a bright-colored strip and notice how they tend to move around the center block.

Octagon Quilt Layout. Scale: 1/4" = 2".

DESIGNING

Additional appliqué may be placed in either the triangular areas in the middle of each side, or in the corners of the second border. All appliqué should be done on the same background fabric.

Although all the quilts shown in this book use my floral appliqué patterns, each is a unique, one-of-a-kind quilt. Each quiltmaker has used the appliqué in her own way to make a personal statement reflecting her particular creative vision. I have designed my book to help you achieve what my students do in my workshops. The guidelines and techniques in this section will help you develop your own floral fantasy.

LETTER TO NANCY

Before you begin exploring the various elements and reach the stage of important decision-making, I thought you might enjoy the story of how one of my very successful students created her floral appliqué medallion quilt. Judy Elwood, of Mount Airy, Maryland, sent me a wonderful letter that is sure to inspire as well as entertain you. Judy's *Black Parrot* quilt is featured on the facing page.

Dear Nancy,

About my quilt, **Black Parrot**, the center block was started in a workshop you taught in Oak Ridge, Tennessee several years ago. You were very generous in sharing your fabric with us, and I distinctly remember my discussing with you the "black print tulips" and saying that I didn't know of any black tulips. You proclaimed that they did not have to be realistic. My "almost finished" block stayed in a drawer for years, and during that time I read in the paper that tulip hybridizers had developed a black tulip. I kept it in my head

Black Parrot by Judy Elwood, Mount Airy, Maryland. 56" x 56".
Collection of Judy Elwood.

that if I ever finished the piece from your workshop, I would look up the name of the black tulip and name my piece the same.

Well, lo and behold, the name I found was Black Parrot. Since the center of the quilt has a red cardinal, I thought it would certainly create some fun and interest to viewers at shows to wonder about the name. And indeed it has!

The small pieced inner border is made from hand-dyed purchased fabrics. I designed the pieced border on graph paper, and I also designed the quilted feather design which is in the cream triangles so that it would fit the area the way I wanted. The feather is stuffed and the background around it is stipple quilted. I designed the appliqué border by using the templates from the center block, adding some shading to leaves to make them appear folded, and adding a "carnation type" flower (lavender or purple) to add more shapes and color. The quilt evolved as it grew from the center out.

There is one solid black tulip dropping over the edge of the upper inner border. This is my tribute to Black Parrot tulips. Thank you for including my quilt in your book.

Judy Elwood

BASIC ELEMENTS

1. *A medallion quilt is planned from the center out.* The rest of the quilt is designed to complement and support this center block. The borders, acting as a frame, complement the picture; they should not compete with the center block.

2. *The overall size of the quilt should not be larger than three times the size of the center block.* Otherwise, the block is not strong enough to carry the larger size of the quilt. If the quilt is too large, the borders overpower and detract from the center block, which needs to be the focal point or visual center of the quilt.

3. *A medallion quilt does not need a lot of borders to be effective.* A strong focal point can be achieved by using a large center, and very little outer border treatment.

4. *The different units of the quilt should relate to one another.* For this reason, it is a good idea to repeat some of the appliqué in the borders. Continuity of design is also maintained by using a similar fabric, such as a *Feature Strip*, to divide the units.

   An additional way to achieve continuity is to repeat similar fabrics, or colors, as the design moves from one unit to another. Notice how the design elements are echoed in my *Techny Chimes* quilt on page 48. The fabrics and colors are repeated even though the appliqué and piecing change.

Flowers and Stars by Ulla Moe, Palatine, Illinois. 48" x 48".
Collection of Ulla Moe.

5. *To make a larger quilt, increase the size of the center block.* The patterns in PART FIVE are designed for a 16" block and can be used as given, or they can easily be enlarged. This can be accomplished by adding more appliqué detail, perhaps a wreath of leaves, or a vine of flower buds around the center floral design.

    The floral block may also be made larger by setting it on a bigger square of slightly darker fabric. Cut the flower block into a large circle, and either appliqué it or reverse-appliqué it onto a slightly darker fabric.

    My Sister's Garden by Lucille Daly, on page 14, illustrates another way to enlarge the center. Lucille combines four blocks into one center unit in order to give the center the necessary size.

NANCY'S HELPFUL HINTS

By keeping the contrast of color stronger in the center block, the focal point becomes more powerful.

BORDER ORGANIZATION

After the size of the center block is chosen, the next step is to plan what will go in the borders. Here are my recommendations for successful borders that are in proportion to the center block:

1. *Always work from the corner to the center of each border.* The corner requires careful planning because the design will be repeated four times. Observe how the corners reach toward each other in my *Techny Chimes* quilt on page 48.

2. *Continue planning the border design until the center of the strip is reached.* The design is then completed. Use a design mirror to visualize the rest of the border.

3. *Borders are usually done in uneven numbers.* A center block with only one border may be complete and ready for the "sandwich" of batting and backing. If additional borders are desired, try three or perhaps five to provide a lovely frame for the center. Lucille Daly uses three borders, two pieced and one appliquéd, in her *Run for the Roses* on page 88.

4. *A series of borders for a large quilt should not overwhelm the center block.* Remember that borders act as support for the center.

Flowers of the Summer Sun center block for a medallion quilt
by Nancy A. Pearson. 28" x 28".

THE CIRCLE WITHIN A SQUARE

When an appliqué design like a spray of flowers is placed within a circle and then the circle is placed within a square, as in the layout on page 72, care must be taken to obtain the proper distribution of space. Here are some considerations for you to incorporate into the planning process:

1. *Decide how large the appliqué design should be compared to the circle.* The appliqué needs to almost fill the circle. If the floral basket sits in the middle of the circle with a lot of open area around it, the basket will appear to be floating in space. Use the **Country Basket** on page 90 as a guide.

2. *Fill up the circle with appliqué, and even let some of the appliqué run over the sides in a few places.* This helps tie the appliquéd circle to the square around it, so that it becomes part of the rest of the quilt. Look at the leaves in **Flowers of the Summer Sun** on page 81.

Sometimes I design and appliqué the center section of my quilt before I decide what I am going to do with it. When I let the design "talk" to me, it begins to grow, one section at a time. While this process is occurring, I try to maintain continuity from one portion of the quilt to the next. Here is a suggestion for maintaining continuity within the quilt:

Carry some of the same fabrics, floral elements and borders from one section to another.

APPLIQUÉ BORDERS

Somewhere among the borders it is necessary to add more appliqué in order to tie the outer area of the quilt to the center block. Here are some design ideas to consider:

1. *Include some of the same flowers from the center block in the border appliqué.* Add some new flowers to create additional interest. Judy Elwood has done this in her **Black Parrot** on page 75. Notice how she appliquéd them in an asymmetric but balanced border arrangement.

2. *The border appliqué should not be so strong that it detracts from the medallion center.* This may be avoided by using colors that are soft, and distributing the appliqué sparingly.

3. *Let the appliqué wander over the edge of the center block, or over the edge of the border, onto other areas of the quilt.* Carrying the appliqué "out and over" the edge helps the border become part of the overall quilt. See how the morning glories spill over from one border to the next in my **Morning Glory** quilt on page 12.

4. *The "out and over" appliqué should be done after the quilt top is assembled.* Then it is easy to determine where the flowers, leaves and vines would be most effective.

NANCY'S HELPFUL HINTS

"Out and over" is one design element you can do with appliqué that you can't do with pieced work, so use it whenever you can. It's really an eye-catcher.

Marian's Rose Basket by Marian Brockschmidt, Springfield, Illinois. 45" x 45".
Collection of Marian Brockschmidt.

PIECED BORDERS

Consider using pieced work somewhere in the borders. The geometric shapes provide a pleasing complement to the curves of the appliqué. Here are some ideas to consider as you begin to design a pieced border:

1. *Include enough detail in the pieced work to balance the detail in the appliqué.* For example, the fan piecing is a nice complement to the wreath and corner appliqués in Grace Pierson's *Tribute to Nancy Pearson* on page 92. Notice how the pieced border balances the appliqué in *Fan and Floral* on page 36.

2. *Fabrics for the pieced border should include some of the colors selected from the Theme Fabric.* You can see how the Theme Fabric is carried from the center basket out to the final pieced border in Marian Brockschmidt's *Marian's Rose Basket* on page 84.

3. *Make a scaled paste-up of the pieced border.* Use a large piece of 1/4" graph paper, and plan as much of the border as you can fit on the paper. Be sure to include the corner, because this is the most important part of the pieced border. Make adjustments to the border at the center of each side, and not at the corners.

   When the paste-up is completed, fit it up against your partial quilt top. Do you like it? Does the corner turn nicely? Make any necessary adjustments. Be careful to keep the borders from overpowering the center.

   The colors of the pieced border in the *Techny Chimes* quilt on page 48 are soft, so that they echo rather than compete with the vibrant flowers in the appliqué. Notice that the inner pieced border design is the center part of the wider outer border, adding to the continuity of the design. The flowers and vines that go "out and over" help tie the entire design together.

OTHER BORDER TREATMENTS

1. *The Plain Fabric Border*. This border provides a nice contrast to the piecing and the appliqué, and gives the eye some relief from all the busy detail. With **Portrait of Summer**, on page 33, Lucille Daly uses wide borders which produce a serene effect.

2. *The Border Print Border*. The discovery of a beautiful border print provides the opportunity to introduce something new to the quilt design. I was pleased to find the elegant border print for my **Poppies** quilt on page 68. A compatible print border also saves time and work.

FEATURE STRIPS

Avoid having borders blend together by using a narrow, contrasting strip of fabric to divide them. I call this piece a **Feature Strip**. When this strip is repeated between the borders, it not only separates them but also adds continuity to the design. You can see the definition that the Feature Strips give to each of the quilt units in **Techny Chimes** on page 48.

Although solid fabrics are commonly used, a narrow, striped fabric from a border print works especially well for a **Feature Strip**. I used a stripe in my **Morning Glory** quilt on page 12. The stripe is printed on the diagonal. When the fabric was cut on the bias and then appliquéd around the large circle on the quilt, the appearance of a circular line was created. See if you can find it. I think it looks great.

If you can't find suitable **Feature Strip** fabrics, try making your own by sewing two or three different fabrics together.

QUILTING DESIGNS

Once you have completed the medallion top, you are ready to plan the quilting design. Be sure to mark the design on the quilt top before you sandwich the layers together. Here are some quilting design ideas that work well to enhance appliqué medallion quilt tops.

1. *Try using some of the flower and leaf shapes from the appliqué as part of the quilting design.* This helps tie the appliqué and the quilting together, lending continuity to the quilt.

2. *Consider using some grid quilting behind the floral shapes.* This is a nice combination because the geometric lines of the grid quilting provide a good contrast to the curves of the quilted floral shapes.

3. *To begin quilting, first outline-quilt around the entire appliqué work.* Place the stitching about 1/8" away from edge of the appliqué pieces. This makes the area puff out more.

4. *Select certain flowers or petals you want to feature.* Quilt around these pieces by placing the line of stitching along the edge of the appliqué so that the stitching defines the shape. This is called *quilting in the ditch*. This method is used to highlight certain areas, and also to hold the fabric sandwich together within the appliqué.

5. *Do not quilt around every individual piece of the appliqué.* When there are many small pieces in the design, too much quilting within the appliqué causes the appliqué fabric to pull and become stiff. It is better to make a careful selection of the pieces to be highlighted. Quilting then functions as an embellishment, bringing the viewer's eye to the featured petals or leaves.

6. *Consider using colored thread.* At the present time I am quilting a piece of appliqué placed on a black background with a violet quilting thread. The effect of the colored thread is especially nice. The color violet also has the advantage of being easy to see on a dark background. Most quilt shops have a good selection of colored threads, so stop by and take a look at them.

Run for the Roses by Lucille Daly, Joliet, Illinois. 86" x 112".
Collection of Lucille Daly.

BINDING

Once the quilting is finished, I know you are anxious to finish the piece with the final step of binding the edges. Don't rush this step! It takes time to do a special job. So much time has been lavished on the appliqué, and now the finishing needs that same extra time and care. You will be glad when you see the final results.

1.   Miter the corners of the binding carefully. This is an important finishing touch.

2.   Consider placing a narrow piping between the binding and the quilted area. This adds a very nice detail to the outer edge of the piece.

DOCUMENTATION

It is important to sign your "masterpiece" with the same care you devoted to the entire project. Place your name and date on the quilt, and also add some of the special things you remember about making it. This information will be greatly appreciated by your family in the years to come.

A quick and easy way to document your quilt is to roll a piece of muslin into a typewriter and type the information you wish to record right onto the fabric. Then appliqué the muslin piece on the back of the quilt. This method provides a way to construct a personal message without any trouble at all.

If you like to embroider, you may want to make a stitched documentation on a separate piece of fabric which is appliquéd to the back of the quilt. Either method insures that this valuable information will remain with the quilt and enhance its value to your family.

Country Basket by Nancy A. Pearson, Morton Grove, Illinois. 18" x 18".
Collection of Nancy A. Pearson.

PART FIVE

PATTERNS: FLORAL FANTASIES

The four patterns in this section feature my original designs for the center block of a floral medallion quilt. The patterns, ranging from easy to complex, may be used as presented, or may be enlarged or altered in any way that meets your creative requirements.

Individual elements may be used as quilting designs, or as appliqué shapes for another project. I hope that you will find these patterns an exciting challenge to stitch. Give them a try, and *enjoy your appliqué!*

POPPIES Gather together lots of bright colored fabrics for the poppies. Brights are important in this pattern. Piece #7 in the large flower lends itself well to a larger print. Cut your template a little deeper in the "U" shaded notches on the leaf. Drawing around the leaf adds size. Clip the seam allowance inside the notched area in wedge shapes.

STAR FLOWERS If you want to make a repeat-block quilt, this pattern works well. It also fits nicely into the *Octagon Quilt* layout. Let the roses in the center carry the brightest color, because that becomes the focal point. Try a *Theme Fabric* in the daisy shapes.

SPRING FANTASY Many favorite spring flowers were chosen for this block. This pattern provides opportunities for lots of color. Remember to give each flower family its own color. Notice the double bar lines on some of the flowers. This is where the *Twisted Fabric* technique is used.

COUNTRY BASKET This pattern offers the opportunity to work with baskets and ribbons. For color choices, refer to the photograph on page 90. Remember to re-mark the pencil lines when they are covered over with another fabric. Use the *Twisted Fabric* technique where you see the double bar lines on the pattern.

Tribute to Nancy Pearson by Grace Pierson, Hinsdale, Illinois. 48" x 48".

ABOUT THE AUTHOR

Nancy A. Pearson is America's foremost designer of original floral appliqué quilts. The beautiful and elaborate designs of her award-winning medallion quilts are the culmination of her training at the American Academy of Art and the School of the Art Institute of Chicago. Prior to her career as an appliqué quilt designer, Nancy worked as a graphic artist for seven years.

The combination of her design background and her quest for fine craftsmanship have garnered many awards for Nancy's quilts. Her meticulous and successful stitching techniques continue to add to her popularity as a workshop instructor and lecturer.

Nancy's most notable prize-winning quilts, recipients of many ribbons, have been widely published and exhibited during the twelve years that she has been teaching quiltmaking. Her ardent admirers throughout the quilt world, who have been clamoring for her to write a book, will be overjoyed to find old favorites and new creations within these pages. Quiltmakers who are meeting Nancy for the first time need only to look at one of her quilts to understand why she holds a place of distinction among fiber artists of the late twentieth century.

TEACHING PLAN

Floral Appliqué lends itself easily to classroom teaching. The following plan incorporates six lessons. You may wish to have longer than one-week intervals between the class sessions. Lessons I through IV focus on creating and stitching the center floral block. Lessons V and VI focus on designing borders and planning the medallion quilt layout.

LESSON I: CREATING A FLORAL BLOCK

Describe the course, and the material to be covered in each class. Begin with the identification of *Theme Fabrics*, showing examples and discussing the reasons for using them. Explain how to determine the focal point of the floral block.

Guide students in assembling fabrics for the flower families, showing how to use fronts and backs of fabrics. Explain "painting with fabric," and why it is necessary to have a large selection of fabrics. Students make a paste-up of a flower, using many values of one color. Suggest making more paste-ups to bring to the next class. Assign the cutting and labeling of templates, the preparation of a background fabric, and the assembling of a basic sewing kit.

LESSON II: PREPARATION AND THE "NO-BASTE" METHOD

Critique the completed paste-ups. Demonstrate what happens when fabrics are moved around within the flower. Introduce the sewing sequence. Guide students through marking the background fabric. Demonstrate cutting and sewing the narrow stems. Students cut out leaves and try the *"No-Baste"* method, followed by the **blind appliqué stitch**. Students select all fabrics and cut the pieces for their projects.

LESSON III: STITCHING TECHNIQUES

Ask students to lay out their projects on the background fabrics. Critique, noting problems and advising solutions. Discuss needle and thread selection.

Supply stitching exercises for narrow stems and leaf points. Demonstrate how to sew one piece over the top of another. Go over the rules for placing greens for stems and leaves. Encourage everyone to complete as much as possible of the floral block. Look for fabrics that might work for framing the finished block.

LESSON IV: STITCHING AND FRAMING

Discuss the addition of embellishment, providing examples of various types. Point out the importance of being accurate.

Supply and begin stitching exercises. If you are teaching beginning or intermediate students, work with inside points and circles. Advanced students may try the **Twisted Fabric** technique. Explain where this technique should be used. Finish appliqué and apply embellishment. Students use selected fabric to frame the block.

LESSON V: PLANNING THE QUILT LAYOUT

Introduce the placement of floral blocks in different medallion layouts as shown in the book. Emphasize choice and possibilities. Discuss the basic rules for designing medallion quilts.

Demonstrate how to lay out the design, using a large sheet of graph paper. Show students how to place the floral block in the center, and then scale the borders. Refer to the layouts in the book, and show how elements can be taken from one layout and combined with elements from another design. Encourage student participation as the complete quilt layout is planned. Have students gather together the fabrics for completing their quilts.

LESSON VI: DESIGNING BORDERS AND FINISHING

Discuss the different types of borders and use of **Feature Strips**. Carefully explain the medallion quilt rules again.

Demonstrate designing an appliqué border with elements taken from the floral center block. Students make a paste-up of a pieced border. Show how color in borders should support the center block, rather than compete with it. Discuss the different styles of quilting patterns. Demonstrate binding, and recommend methods for quilt documentation.

INDEX TO QUILTS AND QUILTMAKERS